I think the series is wonderful and beneficial for tourists to get information before visiting the city.
-Seckin Zumbul, Izmir Turkey

I am a world traveler who has read many trip guides but this one really made a difference for me. I would call it a heartfelt creation of a local guide expert instead of just a guide.
-Susy, Isla Holbox, Mexico

New to the area like me, this is a must have!
-Joe, Bloomington, USA

This is a good series that gets down to it when looking for things to do at your destination without having to read a novel for just a few ideas.
-Rachel, Monterey, USA

Good information to have to plan my trip to this destination.
-Pennie Farrell, Mexico

Aptly titled, you won't just be a tourist after reading this book. You'll be greater than a tourist!
-Alan Warner, Grand Rapids, USA

Thank you for a fantastic book.
-Don, Philadelphia, USA

Great ideas for a port day.
-Mary Martin USA

Even though I only have three days to spend in San Miguel in an upcoming visit, I will use the author's suggestions to guide some of my time there. An easy read - with chapters named to guide me in directions I want to go.
-Robert Catapano, USA

Great insights from a local perspective! Useful information and a very good value!
-Sarah, USA

This series provides an in-depth experience through the eyes of a local. Reading these series will help you to travel the city in with confidence and it'll make your journey a unique one.
-Andrew Teoh, Ipoh, Malaysia

Tourists can get an amazing "insider scoop" about a lot of places from all over the world. While reading, you can feel how much love the writer put in it.
-Vanja Živković, Sremski Karlovci, Serbia

GREATER THAN A TOURIST – SOFIA BULGARIA

50 Travel Tips from a Local

Dimitar Dimitroff

Cover designed by Lisa Rusczyk Ed. D.
Image: https://pixabay.com/en/sofia-central-store-park-bulgaria-1613900/

Greater Than a Tourist
Visit our website at www.GreaterThanaTourist.com

Lock Haven, PA

ISBN: 9781973413202

Dimitar Dimitroff

>TOURIST

50 TRAVEL TIPS FROM A LOCAL

BOOK DESCRIPTION

Are you excited about planning your next trip?

Do you want to try something new?

Would you like some guidance from a local?

If you answered yes to any of these questions, then this Greater Than a Tourist book is for you.

Greater than a Tourist Sophia Bulgaria by Dimitar Dimitroff offers the inside scoop on Sofia. Most travel books tell you how to travel like a tourist. Although there is nothing wrong with that, as part of the Greater Than a Tourist series, this book will give you travel tips from someone who has lived at your next travel destination.

In these pages you'll discover advice that will help you throughout your stay. This book will not tell you exact addresses or store hours but instead will give you excitement and knowledge from a local that you may not find in other smaller print travel books.

Travel like a local. Slow down, stay in one place, and get to know the people and the culture. By the time you finish this book, you will be eager and prepared to travel to your next destination.

TABLE OF CONTENTS

14. TRY RAKIA AND CHASE AWAY THE COLDS

15. DIVE INTO THE LOCAL COFFEE CULTURE

16. SPEED IS ALL YOU NEED

17. "POD LIPITE" - A TEMPTATION FOR THE PALATE

18. KNYAZHEVO – THE WEST GATE OF VITOSHA

19. JHELEZNICA AND THE JACUZZI IN THE FOREST

20. BE A CONQUERER! CHERNI VRAH IS YOUR NEXT GOAL

21. VISIT SOFIA FILM INTERNATIONAL FESTIVAL

22. DISCOVER SOFIA'S HIDDEN CLUBS, PUBS AND BARS

23. LEARN HOW TO DANCE A TRADITIONAL "HORO"

24. CELEBRATE MARCH WITH "BABA MARTA"

25. GRAB A BIKE AND FEEL FREE

26. EXPERIENCE SOFIA'S MOST SPECTACULAR SUNSET

27. "ESCAPE ROOM" CHALLENGE ACCEPTED

28. "SURVA" DEMONS, GO AWAY!

29. SUMMERTIME AND THE LIVING IS EASY

30. WINTER… NOT A BAD SEASON EITHER

31. "LIVE" BEER RIGHT ON THE SPOT

32. NESTINARSTVO - WALKING ON HOT EMBERS

33. PLAY CHESS IN FRONT OF THE NATIONAL THEATER

34. HAVE A PICNIC OR FEED THE SQUIRRELS

35. SHAKE YOUR BODY IN A CHALGA CLUB

36. ROCK THE NIGHT

37. WHICH IS FAVORITE YOUR COLOR?

38. YUMMY! JOIN SOFIA'S FREE FOOD TOUR

39. BRUSSELS ON THE BALKAN PENINSULA

40. BACILLUS BULGARICUS IS THE GERM YOU NEED

41. PLAY BOARD GAMES WITH HEMINGWAY

42. WELCOME TO ROSSO – PAINT AND WINE BAR

43. GO HORSE RIDING AND BREATHE FRESH AIR

44. WHO LET AN ELEPHANT IN THE BOOKSTORE?

45. HAVE A WALK ALONG THE "GRAFA"

46. PAY YOUR HOMAGE TO THE NOBLEST OF ANIMALS

47. TASTE THE GARLIC: TRIPE SOUP

48. PEACE, QUIET, ROWING AND FUN – LAKE PANCHAREVO

49. PAINT EGGS, EAT "KOZUNAK" AND CELEBRATE EASTER

50. SAY "ЧАО" TO SOFIA

TOP REASONS TO BOOK THIS TRIP

> TOURIST

GREATER THAN A TOURIST

> TOURIST

GREATER THAN A TOURIST

NOTES

DEDICATION

This book is dedicated to all the people who helped me come up with great ideas and share them with you. I would like to specifically thank my students who fueled me up with youth power and creativity, and my brother who believed in my ability as a writer and storyteller. To all the great summer nights in our beloved Sofia! Наздраве (Cheers)!

ABOUT THE AUTHOR

Dimitar Dimitroff is a proud Bulgarian who lives in Sofia. He defines himself as an incurable dreamer, explorer and collector of stories.

In his free time, he likes to walk and find new places in the city as well as take his bike and reach destinations no one has told him about. Why? To collect stories. For you.

HOW TO USE THIS BOOK

The Greater Than a Tourist book series was written by someone who has lived in an area for over three months. The goal of this book is to help travelers either dream or experience different locations by providing opinions from a local. The author has made suggestions based on their own experiences. Please do your own research before traveling to the area in case the suggested places are unavailable.

FROM THE PUBLISHER

Traveling can be one of the most important parts of a person's life. The anticipation and memories that you have are some of the best. As a publisher of the Greater Than a Tourist book series, as well as the popular 50 Things to Know book series, we strive to help you learn about new places, spark your imagination, and inspire you. Wherever you are and whatever you do I wish you safe, fun, and inspiring travel.

Lisa Rusczyk Ed. D.
CZYK Publishing

OUR STORY

Traveling is a passion of the "Greater than a Tourist" series creator. Lisa studied abroad in college, and for their honeymoon Lisa and her husband toured Europe. During her travels to Malta, an older man tried to give her some advice based on his own experience living on the island since he was a young boy. She was not sure if she should talk to the stranger but was interested in his advice. When traveling to some places she was wary to talk to locals because she was afraid that they weren't being genuine. Through her travels, Lisa learned how much locals had to share with tourists. Lisa created the "Greater Than a Tourist" book series to help connect people with locals. A topic that locals are very passionate about sharing.

WELCOME TO
> TOURIST

INTRODUCTION

"Many a trip continues long after movement in time and space have ceased." John Steinbeck

Serdica, Constantine the Great's favorite city, stood once where I stand now some two thousand years ago. As much as the city has changed (name, size, population, pretty much everything), it has withstood all the tides of time. From once a Roman city with early Christian basilicas, Roman baths and a spectacular amphitheater to a present-day Sofia – a colorful, lively and bustling city, located between the West and the East. A place where civilizations clashed, fought, won and lost. But most importantly, they left their unique heritage. For me and you. For all of us.

Sofia is like a time traveling machine. When you press one button, you can watch the Ottoman conquest. Then you press another one, and you see people laughing and drinking hot coffee on the high street. Then a third button leads your sight to high-rise buildings and shows you the future. Sofia is not only a bridge connecting the past and the future. It's a diamond absorbing all the colors you can imagine.

All you need is look around. Can you see the green mountain looming above the city. The one that looks like a protective mother embracing her child?

Can you see all the narrow streets and alleys in the city center, covered with cobble stones? This is the heart of contemporary Sofia, beating with the rhythm and pulse of urban culture, carrying the sounds and smells of a city that never sleeps. There you can find nooks which have their stories. Come nightfall, the pulse will start beating faster and faster and a whole new world will open its doors – Sofia nightlife.

Do you know how many parks we have? If the city center is the heart, they are the lungs of Sofia, constantly inhaling gases and negative energy and exhaling precious oxygen and green bliss. There you can do sports, walk your pet, play cards and drink beer with friends, or simply sit on a bench with your loved one with no one around to spoil the moment. What about our customs, traditions and culture? Rich and millennia-old, some of them unique to the region, they will impress and intrigue those who have curious minds. Sofia will turn a mere tourist into a time traveler, explorer and dreamer.

No more talking, let's begin, shall we?

1. WHERE IS SOFIA ON THE MAP

Sofia is the capital of Bulgaria, a country in the European Union, located in southeastern Europe. The country borders Romania, Greece, Turkey, Serbia and Macedonia and the Black Sea. Therefore, you can easily go to other places (Athens, Istanbul, Belgrade). In addition, the Bulgarian seaside is a 3- to 4-hour drive from Sofia.

If you are a citizen of a country part of the EU, you need only have a passport or ID. You won't need a visa or other documents. However, it's advisable to do your research beforehand so that there won't be any problems with your entry.

2. WHAT'S THE OFFICIAL LANGUAGE AND CURRENCY

The official language is Bulgarian, but most young people speak English very well. Those who don't are quite good at body language and make up for not knowing English, so don't worry. The official currency is the Bulgarian Lev (BGN), which you can buy almost anywhere. One of the best places where you can do that is Tavex (they have several offices in Sofia) and offer great exchange rates.

Most probably you will come by plane so when you arrive you can have a taxi or public transportation – buses 84 and 184, which will take you to the city center. The bus fare is fixed 1,60 BGN (approx. $1). There is also a metro station. By using the metro you can access almost all remote districts in the capital (Lulin, Ovcha Kupel, Obelya, Mladost).

3. SLEEP LIKE A CELEBRITY

Once you know where you are heading to, it's good to choose your accommodation. I would recommend several options depending on what you want to experience and your budget.

For those looking for 5-star, world-class performers, I would suggest several hotels – The Hilton, Grand Hotel Sofia, Hotel Marinela and Sense Hotel Sofia with prices ranging from $70 to more than $300 a night.

Of course, there are plenty of 3- and 4-star hotels as well as hostels where one can find a place to sleep for under $20 per night. It really depends on your preferences and whether you want to do more hiking, walking, sports or enjoy the capital's nightlife.

Another option, which I find very appealing when I travel, is to find an individual place on Airbnb. Definitely this is more authentic and original than staying in a hotel since you can choose from a wide range of apartments, houses, lofts, places, areas. You will also individually communicate with your host who might also like to show you around.

For those who want to walk and get lost, you can rent a place on the outskirts - Knyazhevo, Boyana, Simeonovo, Dragalevtsi, which are all huddled at the foot of the mountain and offer fresher air, country-like environment and easy access to green forests.

4. "ЗДРАВЕЙ," HOW ARE YOU?

Can you say that you've been to a place if you don't know how to say hi, cheers and bye?

The Bulgarian language is a beautiful creation; the way it flows and words combine is pure magic. It's also a tough nut to crack. For most foreigners, Bulgarian is quite difficult since we use a different script (English uses the Latin, Bulgarian the Cyrillic script). Often people cannot even read what something says, let alone pronounce it.

Pick any person who can speak English, and they will be happy to teach you some great expressions. Just a few pats on the shoulder from me. The rest is up to you!

"Здравей" or "Здрасти" ("Zdravei" or "Zdrasti") are the two words that mean "Hi" or "Hello". This is how usually people greet each other. You can also say "Добър ден" (Dobar den) which means "Good day to you". "Наздраве" (Nazdrave) is a word you definitely need to know – "Cheers"! I'm sure you will have plenty of occasions where you'll need it. And last but not least, when we end a conversation or when we depart, we say "Чао" (Chao), which means "Bye."

5. SOFIA - A HISTORY LESSON

"Serdica is my Rome"

These are reportedly the words one of the greatest Roman Emperors, Constantine the Great, once said. Serdica is the name of a city dating back to antiquity, or two thousand years ago if we want to be more precise. Following the expansion of the Roman Empire, gradually Serdica became a major economic center, "giving" birth to two emperors –Galerius and Aurelian. -

In the 4th century, Constantine the Great took an immediate liking to the city and even wanted to make it the capital of the Eastern Roman Empire. Unfortunately, that did not happen, and Byzantine was "crowned" and renamed Constantinopole (Istanbul at present). Later, Serdica was sacked by the Huns, restored and renamed Triaditsa.

When the first Bulgarians came to this land in the 8th century, they conquered it and renamed it Sredets. Over the next several centuries the city flourished, even after the Ottoman Empire crashed our Bulgarian ancestors and enslaved our population for almost 500 years. In 1879, Sofia, the new name of the city, became the capital of the liberated third Bulgarian kingdom.

Back in the 19th century, the population was around 11,000 people. The city started quickly to expand following the economic boom of the country. In 1944, after the capital was bombed by both US and UK forces, the city was occupied by the Soviet Army. Today the city is populated by about 1.5 million people.

6. EXPLORE THE CITY'S CHRISTIAN HERITAGE

In the 9th century, Boris I accepted Christianity as the official religion in the country. Ever since then, for more than a thousand years, state and faith have kept the spirit of the Bulgarian people.

The Church of St. George, however, shows that Christianity was here a long time before the 9th century. The church was built around the 4th century and is located in a backyard behind the Presidency building. Not only is the building perfectly preserved, but inside you can see some magnificent frescoes dated back to the 6th century. Outside the church is surrounded by ruins of ancient Serdica.

Another very old church is the symbol of our capital - the Church of Saint Sofia. The building is quite monumental and dates back to the 6th century. The church was so loved that it eventually gave the name of our city.

Alexander Nevsky Cathedral is maybe the most spectacular church in Sofia, a real architectural masterpiece. Built in memory of the Russian soldiers who died in the wars between Russia and Turkey in the 19th century, the building is adorned with mosaics and gold-laden domes that one can even see from Vitosha.

7. TAKE A TOUR AROUND SOFIA'S COMMUNIST PAST

Some 30 years ago, Bulgaria was part of the Eastern Bloc under the influence of the Soviet Union. The period lasted for almost 50 years – from 1944 to 1989. Being a communist country, all colorful, meaningful and artistic things were prohibited. Instead, the country built ugly concrete blocks of flats, which still stand in their glory. You can see them everywhere, especially in neighborhoods like "Lulin" and "Mladost".

There are other monuments which specifically aimed to glorify the image of the socialist worker, or the bravery of the Soviet soldier. The biggest in Sofia, taking up space in of the most beautiful gardens in the capital, is the Monument to The Soviet Army. It was built in 1954 and is a salute to the "saviors" during WWII – The Soviet Army. The monument, nowadays, has become a place where skateboarders practice their stunts and tricks. Occasionally, some of the soldier figures are painted as a form of protest. If you look in the opposite direction, you can see the magnificent building of Sofia University "St. Kliment Ohridski."

Another place where you can learn more about the country's not-so-distant past is the Museum of Socialist Art. Have you wondered why you cannot see Lenin's statues or red stars or other communist symbols? Well, they are all in the museum. It is located in "Mladost" district and you can go there by metro.

8. VISIT THE ONLY FUNCTIONING MOSQUE IN SOFIA

As you know already, Bulgaria has been under Ottoman rule for almost 5 centuries and this has marked the capital's architecture. Unfortunately, most of the mosques, temples where Muslims worship their God, in Sofia were destroyed and only one now exists – Banya Bashi Mosque. Some of the other buildings were transformed into churches.

Built in 1566 on top of thermal springs, the mosque is the only functioning one in Sofia and is the place where the Muslim minority finds peace and solace in their God. It's located opposite Sofia Central Market Hall.

9. "TOUCH" THE GOLDEN TREASURE OF PANAGYURISHTE

This tip will close the chapter "History". If you want to learn more, virtually everything about the country's past and see some unique artifacts, go and visit the National History Museum.

The building is located at the foot of the mountain with a nice backdrop, and the entrance fee is just 10 BGN ($6). Before you even start walking and looking around, you will be awestruck by the massive building of the museum with its high ceilings and chandeliers.

Inside, you have the chance to see the fascinating Thracian golden treasure of Panagyurishte (if it's there because it regularly hits other museums in the world) as well as traditional costume collections. Believe me, it's good value for money.

10. GO ON A SHOPPING SPREE LIKE A BULGARIAN

Maybe before you start exploring the city, you would like to do some shopping. Or maybe after. It entirely depends on you because our malls have nowhere to go!

Sofia is a place where shopping centers flourish. I'm not a huge fan of this procedure, but I know that many people, regardless of gender, indulge in this activity. Our city is absolutely adorable when it comes to places to buy from, and the diversity is phenomenal – from cheap brands to upmarket stores.

To begin with, there is a mall on almost each corner of the city with more popping up by the day. The biggest shopping centers are Serdica Center , The Mall, Bulgaria Mall, Paradise Center, Ring Mall, Mall of Sofia , City Center, Park Center.

Another place you can try is the high street "Vitoshka". It starts from the National Palace of Culture and is a main retail and commercial pedestrian street. On this street you can find some of the best fashion brands as well as bars and pubs.

11. GO GREEN WITH RECYCLED BAGS

Do you want to be green and fashionable at the same time? Well, there is a unique place in Sofia called "Zona Urbana". There are two stores – one on "Angel Kanchev" street and the other one on "Vitoshka". According to their website, "Zona Urbana" is a local manufacturer of bags, wallets, toys and other goods. They are made only of recycled materials and look fabulous. Some of the things are made of old, used newspapers, especially ones from the communist era of the country.

Indeed, every product is unique, handmade and from there you can pick out the perfect souvenir. Your eyes can even spot jewelry and maybe that's the place to purchase a special gift for someone. Also, the store can give you free cartoon maps of Sofia with some amazing places to visit. One shot, two birds.

12. "KILL" YOUR "ENEMIES"

Sofia is a great place to do all sorts of sports and activities. With our malls, parks, sport centers and mountain, this is just the place to stay active and healthy.

One of the funniest and most enjoyable things you can do here is to go and play a game or two of paintball. That is even more tempting if you are a larger group. Instead of playing computer games and live in an artificial world, why don't you "kill" your "enemies" in real life?

There are several places where you can do that. One of them is Paintball Sofia and is in an old building (former factory) on "Nikola Petkov" blvd. I have tried it and it is really nice. Usually (though it depends on how long you play), it will cost you 20-30 BGN ($10-15).

Another place to practice your shooting skills is a club called "Меле" (which means "melee" in English). They organize both indoor and outdoor paintball games.

I'd like to say that everything is safe and secure, so you don't have to worry. However, keep in mind that you will most probably end up having several bruises. But the adrenaline and emotions are worth it.

13. HAVE A TYPICAL BULGARIAN BREAKFAST

The most typical Bulgarian breakfast is a sacred combination of two: "boza" and "banitsa". "Boza" a nutritious fermented beverage made from wheat or millet. The taste is very specific and the drink is thick. Recommendation: buy the smallest bottle possible so that you won't regret afterward. Rumor has it that the beverage helps women enhance their breasts, but I have no idea whether there is any truth to it. Harmonica is a brand that produces organic "boza", and you can buy it from all health food stores in the capital.

"Banitsa"… I remember sending my sister ingredients to Denmark so that she could make one herself. This is how much we love it. It's a type of pastry and the traditional version is with cheese. Also, you can find "banitza" with Turkish delight, pumpkin, apple, spinach and other ingredients. Not only does it taste great but also reminds us of our childhood when we roamed the streets free. You can find it in all bakeries and they are virtually everywhere.

14. TRY RAKIA AND CHASE AWAY THE COLDS

"Rakia – connecting people."

This used be quite the thing some years ago. I still remember people proudly wearing T-shirts with this written on them. Rakia, a traditional alcoholic beverage, has the ability to make you laugh when you want to be serious, to blush when you want to hide your emotions and to dance when you want to quietly enjoy your salad.

Rakia is a fruit brandy and the alcohol content is usually around 40%, so this is no toy to play with. The drink is primarily made of grapes, plums or apricots. However, all sorts of fruits can be used, adding their specific flavor and aftertaste. Some of the best Bulgarian brands are Peshterska, Slivenksa Perla, Sungurlarska, Burgas 63, Kehlibar, Karnobat, but you can find homemade in most open markets in the city. In 2012, "Straldzhanska muskatova" won a third prize in a competition organized annually by the Beverage Testing Institute.

Where can you go and try some rakia? I'd recommend a place which people, both tourists and locals, adore - Rakia Raketa Bar. The place is located on "Yanko Sakazov" blvd opposite park "Zaimov".

The service is excellent and you can try different types of the special, connecting drink. Most people in Bulgaria suggest we combine the drink with salad, in particular "shopska salad". This is my favorite, and it consists of tomatoes, cucumbers and Bulgarian white cheese. You can also try "lukanka" (a unique Bulgarian salami) with it, if you are a meat lover.

Rakia is also used as a medicine when people have fevers, colds or their muscles are stiff. It's also taken as a preventative measure against all things harmful.

15. DIVE INTO THE LOCAL COFFEE CULTURE

"A friend in need is a friend indeed"

In Bulgaria, old and young alike "worship" the black and bitter drink and take it in various forms – with or without milk, cream, sugar, cinnamon, chocolate. You can have it the way you want.

The best places to drink coffee are in the city center. There are basically hundreds of cafés, located on little alleys covered by cobble stones.

Try these: Dabov Speciality Coffee on "Luben Karavelov" street, Chucky's Coffee & Culture and Fabrika Daga. These places take coffee from a mere morning drink to a real pleasure.

16. SPEED IS ALL YOU NEED

You want adrenaline? You want speed? You are a fan of cars and races? Kart racing is one of the many things you can do during your vacation in Sofia.

There are several places, and I will recommend the two I have visited and experienced. The first one is Sofia Karting Ring which is in one of the biggest malls – Sofia Ring Mall. The track is great and the karts are, according to their website, the newest Sodi model. The price is 21 BGN ($12-13) per 10 minutes racing. Pluses: the fanciest place, the newest karts and the best equipment. Minuses – the track is indoors.

The other place I've been to is in "Studentski Grad" neighborhood. Even though the karts are not as new as the ones in Sofia Karting Ring and the quality of the track is not as good, this place is outdoors... you can see the sun or enjoy racing while raining. It's a little cheaper – 18 BGN ($10-11) per 10 minutes.

17. "POD LIPITE" - A TEMPTATION FOR THE PALATE

Time to satisfy your hunger. Bulgarian cuisine is delicious because it combines different influences – local ones, Turkish, Arabic, and the result is fantastic. I will dedicate several tips specifically to some of our delicacies and places to enjoy them.

"Pod Lipite" (which is translated "Under The Linden Trees") is a Bulgarian restaurant, which opened in the distant 1926 and has become a favorite spot for people who want to taste Bulgarian traditional dishes based on authentic recipes. Meat, dairy products, vegetables, the restaurant prides itself on producing them on their own farm. This is a guarantee that the meals will be fresh and tasty.

What can you try? Well, to start with choose a salad- shopska, karakachanska, krasenska and komitska salads. You can also tease your taste buds with the typical Bulgarian white sheep cheese. For the main course, you can choose pork with wild mushrooms or Grafche Tafhche (roasted beans). There are also other vegetarian dishes. For a dessert you can have a homemade yogurt or banitza with Turkish delight; whichever you choose, you won't regret it.

Sometimes there are events when live music (traditional) and dances are performed. You can even try to learn how to dance.

18. KNYAZHEVO – THE WEST GATE OF VITOSHA

This place has a soft spot in my heart because I have lived here for the last year. In my opinion, this is the "wildest" and most beautiful neighborhood in Sofia. Why?

Well, the district is located at the foot of the mountain, our beloved Vitosha. At the same time, it's connected with the city center directly by tram number 5, which is the oldest tram line in the city. In the beginning of 20th century, Knyazhevo was the Beverly Hills of Sofia - a place where politicians, the rich and the famous had their summer villas. There was also a public bath (which is abandoned now but still can be seen) with mineral water. The bath is believed to have existed thousands of years ago, used by the ancient Thracians who populated these lands before the Romans came.

Residents of the city come here for two main reasons: to go hiking and to pour some mineral water.

Regarding the former, I want to say that the route from this side of the mountain is the most suitable for all age groups – it's not as steep as the other routes. This is the reason why at weekends, Knyazhevo is like a market place with all the hundreds and thousands of people coming. From Knyazhevo you can follow the route to Cherni Vrah, which takes 3-4 hours. The forest above Knyazhevo consists mainly of pine trees, and the air smells of resin.

People can have water from several places in Knyazhevo. The one that people use the most is at the last tram stop in Knyazhevo.

19. JHELEZNICA AND THE JACUZZI IN THE FOREST

Nowadays, people are ready to pay an arm and a leg just to have a single SPA procedure. In a hotel. In a room. In Jheleznica, there is no need to pay. Besides, you can have all the space, the sky and the stars while relaxing in the warm, mineral water.

Jheleznica is some 20 km away from Sofia, and by car the journey takes less than half an hour. There is also public transportation – buses number 98 and 67. After the bustling city, Jheleznica strikes the visitor as a calm and quiet place with nice-looking houses, gardens full of crops (assuming it's in the summer) and friendly people who would love to give some instructions.

The "jacuzzis" are in the forest, a 15-minute walk from the center of the village. These pools are filled with warm (around 30 °C) water coming from underground springs. There are three groups of pools located on different spots in the forest. The first one and closest to the village is even inside a building. The other ones are outdoors and, believe me, there's nothing like it when you are inside the warm water and all around you is pure whiteness made of snow. In the summer, the air is cool and the mountain protects you from the blazing sun.

From Jheleznica you can also go hiking and top some of the peaks as well as reach two other destinations – Bistrica and Pancharevo.

20. BE A CONQUERER! CHERNI VRAH IS YOUR NEXT GOAL

If you are planning to come to Sofia, you have to conquer the highest peak in Vitosha – Cherni Vrah (translation "Black Peak"). Reaching 2290m, the peak is the fourth highest in the country.

From my perspective, the main purpose of trying to climb a mountain is not reaching the summit, but rather joining forces with nature. Understand the real definition of "quiet", hear the wind rustling and every leaf falling down, find the best views and contemplate our existence. If you reach the peak, that's even better.

There are perhaps more than 20 different routes that lead to Cherni Vrah. You can attempt to climb it from Knyazhevo, as you already know, Boyana, Dragalevtzi, Simeonovo, Jheleznica, Bistrica and even Vladaya (a village close to Sofia). Those who are better trained and fitter usually start from places at the foot of the mountain, while others take a bus or a gondola lift (there are several) and reach higher destinations from where they start climbing. Wrap yourself warmly because even in summer, the mountain shows its white teeth.

Once you reach the top, you can enjoy all the views – Rila mountain and Stara Planina (translated "Old Mountain"). In addition, there is a hut from where you can have a tea or something warm to eat.

21. VISIT SOFIA FILM INTERNATIONAL FESTIVAL

Sofia Film Fest is the biggest film festival in Bulgaria and is an annual event. Next year, the fest will last from the 8th -18th March. By attending the fest, you will have the rare opportunity to watch local films with subtitles. In addition, artists from 50 countries take part in the event and make it even more colorful.

22. DISCOVER SOFIA'S HIDDEN CLUBS, PUBS AND BARS

Sofia Pub Crawl is the best way to discover the city's hidden pubs and bars! By walking around, you will have the chance to enter places you didn't even know existed. Moreover, you will have company – people from all around the world as well as nice locals who will be your guides.

The price of the tour is fixed 20 BGN ($12-13), and this will guarantee some free drinks in some of the places you visit. There are no certain destinations to visit; they differ depending on the day or the size of the group. Every day people meet at 9pm at Park Crystal, and from there they start walking and looking for the "secret" gems of the city.

23. LEARN HOW TO DANCE A TRADITIONAL "HORO"

Bulgaria's folk dances are an inseparable part of our cultural and national heritage developed in the span of centuries. Our folklore has captured the very soul of the Bulgarian man – our hardworking and free nature.

During the Ottoman rule (from 1396 to 1878), our people had little comfort, and they found it in singing and dancing. Depending on the region where they come from, the typical "horo" varies significantly, reflecting the temperament of the people who have lived there for centuries – fast, slow, cheerful, graceful, "heavy" and many more. The diversity and complexity are incredible.

Billy Dance and Sport Center is a dance academy that helps people learn how to dance traditional "hora". Keep in mind that these dances are sometimes really difficult to perform, though the professionals do it effortlessly. The academy offers a one-day visit which will cost you 7 BGN ($4). For just a day, you can feel the tempo and energy, however, it's highly unlikely to master any of them.

If you are visiting Bulgaria during the New Year Celebrations, once the clock strikes 12 and people drink a glass of champagne, we form one very long "horo" and dance more than 10 minutes. This is the so-called "pravo horo" and is relatively easy to learn.

24. CELEBRATE MARCH WITH "BABA MARTA"

When 1st March comes, we celebrate "Baba Marta" (translation "Grandma Marta"). We buy a "martenitsa" for every person we hold dear. Each "martenitsa" is made of red and white yarn, which are intricately interwoven. The most common ones are bracelets which we wear on our wrists (sometimes people have 20-30.)

The white color is a symbol of purity and beauty as well as innocence, while the red symbolizes health, love and strength. We have to carry them until we see a stork or a blossoming tree.

If you are interested, there are workshops where you can create "martenitsa" of your own.

25. GRAB A BIKE AND FEEL FREE

Sofia Free Bike Tour is yet another awesome opportunity for tourists to experience the city in another way – on a bike.

The tour is organized throughout the whole year and for the period between November and April, you need to make a reservation first. From May to October, you just have to show up at the arranged hour and place – the imposing "Ivan Vazov" National Theatre. A local guy will show you around the most famous landmarks in the city.

It's important to say that if you don't have a bike, you have to rent one for 10 BGN($6). You can also use an electric bicycle, but the price is higher – 28 BGN ($16-17).

26. EXPERIENCE SOFIA'S MOST SPECTACULAR SUNSET

If you are a sunset hunter, or a nature lover, or just an incurable romantic, try the Vitosha Sunset Tour. The good thing about it is that there are organized all year round regardless of the season. Since it depends on the weather conditions, you have to book a reservation first.

The place where you gather is the "Ivan Vazon" National Theater and the group leaves about 2.5 hours before sunset. The price of the tour is 40 BGN ($24) and it does not include transportation.

Once the group is ready they set off and go by taxi to Aleko Hut in Vitosha. From there, people should hike to the final destination – Kamen Del Peak , where the view of the city is breathtaking. After the sun goes down and darkness descends, the group will go back the same way they have come.

27. "ESCAPE ROOM" CHALLENGE ACCEPTED

Is your mind constantly working? Do you think you are a walking genius? Do you feel challenged when someone tells you "You cannot solve that?" The "Escape Room Challenge" series is then for you! These are rooms in the city center where people enter and to try to get out in 60 minutes. In Sofia there are 79 Escape Rooms at present.

3 Key Room "The Detective and the Time Machine" is the first one I suggest. A team of 2-6 people will be locked for 60 minutes. You will be given lots of clues and provoked into solving mysterious puzzles. Can you find the way out? The room is on "Vasil Levski" blvd.

The next room I recommend is "Hour Escape" and its description is "no doors, no windows, no way to get out." Sounds exciting! Another one is the series "Teorema Rooms" with their two rooms "T.N.T" and "Atlantis". You can visit their website and book one of the rooms.

28. "SURVA" DEMONS, GO AWAY!

In January and February each year, all around the country a special celebration takes place. This is an old and pagan custom to chase away the evil spirits and welcome the upcoming spring. The custom celebration is called "kukeri" (mummers) and for the occasion people wear terrifying masks and elaborate costumes.

"Surva" is an annual "kukeri" festival in Pernik, which is some 20-30 km away from Sofia. Thousands of people from all around the country gather and perform their region's masquerade games. The dances are a mystic unity of rhythm, sound and color. Usually, the performers wear several big bells that tinkle all the time while jumping and walking around. Not only can you watch and drink some wine but also participate in the games. All you need is a good mood and a scary mask.

Next year, the event will last from 26-28 January.

29. SUMMERTIME AND THE LIVING IS EASY

Our summers are long, sunny and hot. What can one do when there's plenty of sunshine? Why don't you go to a swimming pool?

"Dianabad" is the biggest complex with three swimming pools. This year everything was renovated, and now the pools don't look like the ones they used to be in 1989. It's great because there is a lot of free space in and out of the pool and it won't be necessary to rub someone's back for a spot. Inside the complex there is also a bar with cool cocktails, food, and you can even smoke hookah . The entrance fee is 10BGN ($6) for adults.

Another place to visit is a swimming pool "Leda". A sweet escape from the heat, Leda offers reasonable prices, and at night also attracts visitors with its hip-hop and foam parties.

"Villa Spaggo" is a complex located outside of village Bistrica. You will be surround by the green looming mountain, summer fields and gently rolling hills. The Villa has a hotel and a nice restaurant tempting with Italian cuisine. Adjacent to the restaurant and the hotel is the swimming pool, which you can enjoy from June to the end of September depending on the weather.

30. WINTER... NOT A BAD SEASON EITHER

Winter always comes. Summer lovers like me are never happy, but many people enjoy the coziness of the winter months. Usually, we have winters with low temperatures and plenty of snow and it lasts from the end of November to March.

If you plan to visit Sofia in the winter, except for the other things you can try (excluding the summer activities), there are plenty of things to indulge in. One of them is skiing.

Not only does Vitosha give amazing views and leisurely walks in the pine forest but also turns into a ski resort in winter. There are more than 20 km of ski slopes both for skiing and snowboarding. If you like night skiing, there is an option to do so.

Another thing you can do is take your friends and go ice-skating. There are several ice rinks and one of them is "Slavia" (next to Slavia Stadium). "Ariana" (next to "Vasil Levski" National Stadium) is an open-air rink, and after 18:00 there is usually a DJ party.

31. "LIVE" BEER RIGHT ON THE SPOT

One of the things every tourist should try is the local beer or go to a place where beer is worshiped.

Just like most European countries, in Bulgaria we love to drink the cool liquid, especially when it's summer and we are outside with friends. However, it's also a good way to spend a cold January night in a place where you can pour the beer yourself. Does that sound interesting to you?

If it does, go and visit AleHouse on "Hristo Belchev" street. You can have beer right on the spot, the very table you are sitting at. Next to the table you will find a metered tap, which you can use to pour as much you'd like to drink. According to their website, the "live" beer they offer is "unfiltered, unpasteurized, containing no preservatives." Other places worth mentioning are – "Kanaal" and "Na Popa" which offer a wide range of beers.

The most common Bulgarian brands are Zagorka, Shumensko, Kamenitza, Burgasko, Pirinsko, Ariana. However, though it's not as popular as the others, the classiest of them all is Stolichno. Personally, I love this beer, especially the dark one. Also, if you can find a local beer called White Stork, don't think twice.

32. NESTINARSTVO - WALKING ON HOT EMBERS

Part of UNESCO Intangible Cultural Heritage Lists, "nestinarstvo" (walking on embers) is an ancient fire walking ritual performed in a few villages in Bulgaria and northern Greece. The right to perform the fire ritual have only people who have inherited the gift from their ancestors. It's a mystery how these people walk barefoot on the hot coals without any damage to their skin.

On 20th May this year, for the first time in Sofia a fire festival with four bonfires took place. The event warmed up the guests with folk dances and songs and the highlight of the night was walking on hot embers. The people who have organized the fest hope that it will become an annual event and tourists can visit it in Sofia.

33. PLAY CHESS IN FRONT OF THE NATIONAL THEATER

"Ivan Vazov" National Theater is one of Sofia's major landmarks and has an imposing building with golden elements and architecture that will take your breath away. Named after the patriarch of Bulgarian literature, Ivan Vazov, the theater is currently the biggest and the oldest in the country. The interior has been recently renovated and is a piece of art itself.

The garden in front of the building is the oldest city garden and has benches for the people to sit down, and also a beautiful fountain. Sometimes there are live concerts there, but usually this is a place with its own subculture. Many young people gather there, drink beer, play cards, do sports – badminton, for example.

Just next to the fountain, you will see "tables" where people can play "outdoors" chess. The people playing there seem to be having the time of their lives. They are so passionate and engrossed, with crowds surrounding them, that they seem to live in a world of their own. So if you are a chess fan, you can sit down and play with someone. You can even bet and earn some money.

34. HAVE A PICNIC OR FEED THE SQUIRRELS

There are four main parks in Sofia and all of them are green and lovely.

South Park has a special place in my heart since I almost grew up there. Basically you can do all sorts of things – walk your dog, run and do some exercise, have a picnic on the green lawns. If you take a walk, most probably you will notice that there are many squirrels in the trees. These brown cuties are often not afraid of people and sometimes climb down and wait for a special treat. What can you give them? Well, these friendly animals love different types of seeds and nuts – peanuts, corn, walnuts and, of course, acorns.

In South Park you can also rent a rickshaw (without a driver!) or play table tennis.

The other three parks are West Park, Park "Borisova Gradina" and North Park. They are all very different from each other and have their own story to tell.

35. SHAKE YOUR BODY IN A CHALGA CLUB

Chalga, which is often called pop-folk, is one of those genres that almost no one admits to listening to, but almost everyone actually does. It's very common in Bulgaria.

Chalga music has its own subculture in the country – it promotes inappropriate behavior, nakedness and fake, plastic, untalented singers. But for people who don't live here and don't understand the lyrics, it could mean another bombastic night in Sofia.

If I have to be honest, I have never met a foreigner who hasn't liked it. The way outsiders see things is different; after all they are on holiday here. I agree that chalga parties are wild, crazy and noisy. People have so much fun. Which are the best places to try your luck?

Some of the most popular clubs are in "Studentski Grad" (translated "Students' Town) because students are known for their sleepless nights (anything but studying, right?) and are always in a mood for fun. Club 33 and The Cotton Club are the two hot spots. Plaza Dance Center is also a place you might visit.

36. ROCK THE NIGHT

If chalga is not for you, then check out these rock clubs.

Rock'n'Rolla is considered to be the best rock club in town by both locals and foreigners. The club has a capacity of 500 people and on Fridays and Saturdays, it's jam-packed. Depending on the night, the music ranges from pop-rock and classics like AC/DC and Nirvana to heavy metal. What's more, there is a separate karaoke room. There you can meet happy young people from here and also a many tourists. The club is located on "Graf Ignatiev" street

RockIt is another shelter for those who like heavier music. At and after midnight, this place is Sofia's hell. The music is loud and powerful and everyone's just jumping, screaming and drinking tons of beer. You can also order food as well as play billiards and table football. Sometimes they have live performances by Bulgarian rock and metal bands, and then all hell breaks loose.

37. WHICH IS FAVORITE YOUR COLOR?

Which is your favorite color? Well, if you join the annual celebration of the Festival of Colors that will not matter at all! The fest has been organized every year ever since it first kicked off in 2014.

The date is not fixed, but it is usually when summer begins (in June), so the weather is warm, humid and everything is lush and green. The venue changes annually, and the people who attend the festival can buy bags with different powders in different colors. Then the fun begins when all the bags are torn and thrown, and all the multitudes become one messy and laughing rainbow.

During the party, you will have the chance to listen to live music as well as engage in other things, such as fun activities, workshops and Indian customs and dances.

38. YUMMY! JOIN SOFIA'S FREE FOOD TOUR

Is there a greater way to spend an afternoon in an unknown place than having a few bites of national cuisine? I think not!

Balkan Bites is the organization that is behind the tour. It attempts to show tourists some of the most attractive family-owned restaurants in Sofia. There, people can try some traditional Bulgarian food as well as hear more about the customs and the history. The tours are guided by professionals, so everything will be arranged and explained.

Where's the meeting point? Well, every day at 14:00 in front of the statue of Stefan Stambolov (Park Crystal). The tour lasts around 2 hours and the food is free. No taxis or transport, everything is on foot so that you can contemplate and digest at the same time.

"Mekitsa and Coffee" is just one of the places to visit where you can have the traditional "mekitsa" (fried pastry) and hot coffee. Most of us grew up eating grandma's "mekitsa" at weekends. It brings sweet memories and new experiences for those who have never tried it.

39. BRUSSELS ON THE BALKAN PENINSULA

Brussels is famously known for its chocolate shops. I myself remember the beautiful chocolate figures when I visited the Belgian capital. However, I could only look and admire.

In Sofia, people also value the qualities of chocolate, especially one made with love, professionalism and care. One of the brands that offers Belgian chocolate produced in Bulgaria is Valentino Chocolatier. Currently, they have three Chocolate Houses in the capital. One of them is on "Patriarh Evtimii" blvd in the city center. One more thing – they offer beers that can go with the sweet treat. I find this combination exquisite.

"Gorchivosladko" is a boutique bakery that produces Italian style chocolate. It's also in the city center on "Gladstone" street. Other places chocolate lovers might visit are Chocol'art, Amelie and Venchi.

40. BACILLUS BULGARICUS IS THE GERM YOU NEED

If there is a thing that can make a Bulgarian proud, this is the Bulgarian yogurt. Creamy, thick and delicious it is considered to be the healthiest of all dairy products. Why is it so special?

Well, to call yogurt Bulgarian it needs to contain two specific microorganisms, and one of them is Bacillus Bulgaricus. These two bacteria are the main "culprits" for the taste, thickness and properties. Bulgarian yogurt is a natural probiotic and helps alleviate stomach and intestinal problems.

Yogurt is usually made from cow milk, goats milk and even (the most delicious one) buffalo milk. When you add strawberry jam, it becomes the perfect dessert.

41. PLAY BOARD GAMES WITH HEMINGWAY

If only Hemingway was alive, I'd be the first person to go there and talk to the man. But his spirit is not dead. He lingers in "Studentski Grad" neighborhood and, more precisely, in Hemingway's Board Game Café.

The café has more than 200 board games and you can enjoy rock or jazz music while playing. The staff will help with some of the games you don't understand and give a fresh beer for an even better mood.

42. WELCOME TO ROSSO – PAINT AND WINE BAR

Bulgaria has a mild and lovely climate which is the reason why my people have grown high-quality grapes for centuries. Consequently, they turned them into a variety of wines – rich and fruity. The most pleasant way to discover the properties of the Bulgarian wine is while painting a picture.

Bar Rosso is the first bar in the country where you can draw and have a glass of classy wine at the same time. Local artists will show you a step-by-step tutorial on how to paint your picture, and a wine expert will talk about the different wines they offer and their qualities. This just the place for creative and artistic folks.

43. GO HORSE RIDING AND BREATHE FRESH AIR

Do you like horses? Have you ever ridden one of these magnificent animals? You can try it during your vacation in Sofia.

One of the best places is EzdaSofia and their stable is in Dragalevtsi district. One of their best offers is 20 hours of horse riding for 150 BGN ($80-90). In addition, you can go and feed the animals after training – bring carrots, apples or sugar lumps. EzdaSofia's clients can also celebrate their birthdays and other special occasions.

Another place is Adgor, after Jheleznica, and they claim that they use a technique called "natural horsemanship". The place where the stable is located is pristine and the air is purified by four mountains – Vitosha, Rila, Verila and Plana.

44. WHO LET AN ELEPHANT IN THE BOOKSTORE?

Many people are huge fans of reading and cannot imagine their holidays without the touch of a book and the nice aroma of pages. Since most bookstores offer literature in Bulgarian, this will not be of great help to you as a tourist. Yes, most shops have English books, but the diversity is not phenomenal. But… there is one special place you can visit and leave with a happy and fluttering heart.

It is called "Elephant Bookstore" or Sofia's English Bookshop as we local folks know it. An incredible place! This is a vintage, second-hand bookshop. The atmosphere is artistic and the people who work there are friendly. The shop boasts 10,000 titles, including Bulgarian authors translated into English.

45. HAVE A WALK ALONG THE "GRAFA"

One of the most romantic streets in the city center is the so-called "Grafa". The whole name of the street is "Graf Ignatiev", and it starts from "Vitoshka" and reaches "Evlogi Georgiev" blvd.

The street is a place where many people shop for clothes, shoes, bags or books, and also there are many nice cafés and restaurants. While walking, especially in autumn, you can stop at a stand where people sell roasted chestnuts (very delicious) or roasted pumpkin with honey and walnuts. Take those treats to the little garden with benches in front of the "Sveti Sedmochislenici" Church and enjoy the warm and peaceful days of autumn.

46. PAY YOUR HOMAGE TO THE NOBLEST OF ANIMALS

"A lion is called 'a king of beasts' for a reason"
Jack Hanna

The Lion. The proudest and noblest of animals is Bulgaria's national symbol. Historically speaking, the lion has been a heraldic symbol of Bulgaria since the 13th century. It represents our strength and freedom.

Statues of the great beast are everywhere in the capital – from "Lavov Most" (this means Lion's bridge) and in front of the Sofia Court House to the recently restored monument in front of the National Palace of Culture.

The statue spent decades in a museum before it was exhibited again in front of the eyes of locals and foreigners. In 1980, it was replaced by a monument, which no one knew what it was and what it meant. Fortunately, the statue of the lion is back where it belongs. Not only is it a symbol of our country and people, but also the monument commemorates those who died in the Balkan Wars and World War I.

47. TASTE THE GARLIC: TRIPE SOUP

I cannot think of anything more traditional, more Bulgarian and more… garlic than a tripe soup! As one person has said: We are all equal before a bowl of tripe soup. He is right since I have seen both homeless and rich eat it with such pleasure and gusto.

The soup is made of tripe (usually from a cow) and milk. Most people love to put garlic sauce inside, which makes it quite smelly and, apparently, attractive. It's also considered to be a cure for hangover. So if you have drunk a little too much rakia, go to "Divaka" and enjoy a tripe soup.

"Divaka" is a brand with three restaurants in the city center. They will serve you one of the best tripe soups in the capital.

48. PEACE, QUIET, ROWING AND FUN – LAKE PANCHAREVO

Lake Pancharevo is an artificial lake located on the outskirts of Sofia, between two mountains Vitosha and Lozenska. There are very many beautiful paths around the lake where you can have a stroll and breathe clean air while watching the scenery. Beside the lake there is a park which people use for a weekend picnic or barbecue. I also recommend you visit a spa complex "Korali" that has a swimming pool filled with hot spring water (49 degrees).

But if you have decided to be active, you can rent a boat or a pedalo. Keep in mind that swimming in the water is forbidden, so don't do it. However, fishing is not and many people fish there every day.

49. PAINT EGGS, EAT "KOZUNAK" AND CELEBRATE EASTER

Spring has come. Birds are twittering and playing hide-and-seek. Everything is ready to explode with joy and life. This period is often marked by one of the most sacred and loved Christian celebrations – Easter.

Bulgaria adheres to the Orthodox Faith, which in many ways differs from both Catholicism and Protestantism. First of all, our Easter is on a different date. In addition, we have some customs and traditions typical for the region – painting eggs and eating "kozunak".

The more colorful the eggs are, the better. However, the first one should always be red. The process of dying could happen only on a Thursday or Saturday before Easter. "Kozunak" is a Bulgarian Easter bread, which might contain raisins or Turkish delight. On Easter Sunday, we wake up and start cracking the eggs, and then we have breakfast with them and the "kozunak".

50. SAY "ЧАО" TO SOFIA

Time to say goodbye! I'm sure you will be full of sweet memories and great experiences to tell your grandchildren one day. On the other hand, maybe it's a good idea to buy something to remind you of Sofia and Bulgaria.

One of the things is rose oil. Bulgaria is one of the biggest producers, certainly exporting the one with the highest quality. In all souvenir shops you can find little bottles with rose water (rose oil is extremely expensive).

You can also buy pottery or ceramics, which you can use to cook something when you go home.

"Balkansko" is a souvenir shop on "Vitoshka" that offers incredible items – ceramics, wooden souvenirs, copper items, leather products, icons, textile and more.

TOP REASONS TO BOOK THIS TRIP

Historical Sites: They are basically everywhere. Look to the right – a communist monument, turn left – an old Roman church. Sofia is built on history.

Sports: The capital is a great place for an active holiday – skiing, snowboarding, cycling, paintball, karting, running. The list is endless.

Nightlife: There is a whole palette of clubs, bars, discos, pubs where you can listen to rock, jazz, pop, chalga, hip-hop. Anything you enjoy.

Food: Bulgarian cuisine is influenced by many cultures and is a mixture of delicious dishes.

Culture: From the masquerade games to the fire walking rituals, Bulgaria's cultural heritage is unique.

> TOURIST
GREATER THAN A
TOURIST

Visit GreaterThanATourist.com:

http://GreaterThanATourist.com

Sign up for the Greater Than a Tourist Newsletter:

http://eepurl.com/cxspyf

Follow us on Facebook:

https://www.facebook.com/GreaterThanATourist

Follow us on Pinterest:

http://pinterest.com/GreaterThanATourist

Follow us on Instagram:

http://Instagram.com/GreaterThanATourist

> TOURIST GREATER THAN A TOURIST

Please leave your honest review of this book on Amazon and Goodreads. Thank you.

We appreciate your positive and negative feedback as we try to provide tourist guidance in their next trip from a local.

NOTES

Made in the USA
Las Vegas, NV
01 September 2022

54542571R00052